THE "ME" PROJECT

Be/Become Who You Are

12-WEEK JOURNAL & PLANNER

RESONANCE WITHIN, LLC.

THE "ME" PROJECT: Be/Become Who You Are

HOV Publishing is a division of HOV, LLC.
Bridgeport, CT 06605
Email: hopeofvision@gmail.com

Cover Design and Layout: HOV Designs
Editors: Kecia "Sissy" Lucas and Sister Kimberly Muhammad

Contact the Author:
Resonance Within, LLC
Karen Taylor Muhammad
resonancewithin.ktm@gmail.com

For further information regarding special discounts on bulk purchases, please contact: Karen Taylor Muhammad at resonancewithin.ktm@gmail.com

ISBN Hard case: 978-1-955107-56-3

Printed in the United States of America

Peace and Blessings to all!

My purpose in creating The "ME" Project stems from my guidance, inspiration and motivation through life encounters and experiences; in which it was shared and supported by my loving family.

My support system are my parents: Marion E. Taylor (mother) and Calvin Taylor Jr. (father - June 10, 1938 - May 20, 2020); siblings: Calvin Taylor III (brother) and Donna R. Taylor (sister in law), Kecia "Sissy" Lucas (sister), and Kristi Taylor Durham (sister - February 11, 1969 - February 19, 2021) and Earl Quan Durham (brother in law- July 19, 1971 - February 1, 2022); nephews: Karriem R. Harris, Quentin J. Harris, Dustin W. Hayes; nieces: Diedra R. Hayes, Cheyenne T. Bittle, Kyra Q. Durham and a host of cousins and friends.

My spiritual foundation, which I am grateful, is through the Nation of Islam (NOI), The Honorable Minister Louis Farrakhan (THMLF), The Honorable Elijah Muhammad (THEM), Muslim Girl Training and General Civilization Class (MGT & GCC), Crossfit DGA, and former spouses.

I would like to thank you, the readers, for being on this journey with me and The "ME" Project. The "ME" Project has allowed me to become the person, whom, I have always desired to become and to grow through deeper meaning and understanding.

My sincere appreciation and gratitude is to Allah (God) who continually provides.

May Allah grant us peace and protection.

Salaam/Peace 🖤

"Stop looking for things in others, I'm not willing to give myself. Everything I desire is within, waiting to be discovered, by ME."

TABLE OF CONTENTS

"To realize one's destiny is a person's only real obligation."

~ Paulo Coelho
The Alchemist

1. JOURNAL USE INSTRUCTIONS

1.1. **Resonance Within** is to BE/BECOME WHO YOU ARE.

1.2. **What is the meaning of Resonance?**

The word resonant means a deep resonant voice, clear and loud with a lasting effect within oneself.

When that inner voice resonant with you, it elevates you on an emotional level where one can relate. It moves through you and evokes a feeling of familiarity. On some occasions, it may even inspire you to take action.

This is the intention of The "ME" Project, to inspire you to take action into Be/ Become (Ing) WHO YOU ARE− for The Creator, Allah (God), created His Creation, in His likeness and His image.

1.3. **Physics & Definition of Resonance:**

A phenomenon, in which, an external force or a vibrating system, forces another system around it to vibrate, with greater amplitude at a specified frequency of operation.[1]

---

[1]https://byjus.com/physics/resonance/#:~:text=What%20is%20resonance%20in%20Phy sics,a%20specified%20frequency%20of%20operation.

> If You Correct Your Mind, The Rest of
> Your Life Will Fall Into Place ~Lao Tzu

1.4. What is the "ME" Project?

The "ME" Project is a 12-Week Journal & Planner to help you BE/BECOME WHO YOU ARE.

The 3 main elements (listed below), will initiate a starting point on your ME journey. It will aid you to reach your true and authentic Self:

S = Spiritual

M = Mind/ Mental

B = Body/ Physical

> "The "ME" Project, is you and you atoning with you. Face yourself!"
> ~ Sister Stacey L. Muhammad

1.5. Transformation Challenge

The 12-Week Journal & Planner is to develop and provide awareness in the different areas of self.

The 12-week cycles are:

- **Self**-Love
- **Self** -Awareness
- **Self** -Esteem
- **Self** -Discipline
- **Self** -Control & Unity

> To SEARCH WITHIN SELF and UNVEIL/ REVEAL the TRUE "ME".
> ~ Karen Taylor Muhammad

1.6. The "ME" Project Community

The "ME" Project Community is designed to promote:

- Growth
- Development
- Accountability
- Community

Common + Unity = Community

The commonality is we all have encountered & experienced trials, tribulations, and the vicissitudes of life (heartache, pain, loss, disappointment, and frustration) as girls, boys, sisters, brothers, women, men, mothers, fathers, wives, and husbands. We have voices that need to be expressed through positive, constructive, conducive means to BE/ BECOME WHO WE WERE CREATED TO BE. In our unity, there is POWER to move mountains WITHIN and WITHOUT.

1.7. Community

There are 9 systems in the body, the 10th system being the brain. If one of the systems is out of sync (ill or dysfunctional) then the body is not in harmony with itself; therefore, the unity within the body is out of communication. (For more clarity on the 10 Systems of A Universal Order, read page xvi)

"100% dissatisfaction brings about 100% change."
~ The Honorable Elijah Muhammad

1.8. What Can Be Achieved Through The "ME" Project?

- Prayer = Spirit
- Study/Reading/Reflection = Mind
  (Daily reading of The Holy Quran, The Holy Bible or The Torah (Pentateuch)).
- Workout = Body/ Physical
- Mediation/ Journaling = S.M.B. Connection
  (see 1.3) or to expound on what the daily Quranic, Biblical or Pentateuch verse(s) reveal(ed) to you & what you are feeling.

1.9. Essay

Who you are now and who you would like to be at the end of the 12-Weeks / 3-Month cycles.

- **1ST Challenge**: Your 1st 12-Week / 3 Month Cycle
  - At the end of your Transformation cycle, submit to yourself essay and photos.

- **2ND Challenge:** Your 2nd 12-Week / 3 Month Cycle
  - At the end of your Transformation cycle, submit to yourself essay and photos.

- **3RD Challenge:** Your 3rd 12-Week / 3 Month Cycle
  - At the end of your Transformation cycle, submit to yourself essay and photos.

"One who seeks to control others has no self-control."
~ Karen Taylor Muhammad

2. RESONANCE TIPS

2.1.   What is Meditation?

Mediation is a way to quiet the mind outwardly to look within.

2.2.   What is Appreciation?

Appreciation affords you the opportunity to be present in that very moment, the rewards are instant and continuous.

How many moments are you missing?

_____

_____

_____

_____

Where are you NOW in your development? Are you in the past, present, or future.

_____

_____

_____

_____

"If you are depressed you are living in the past. If you anxious you are living in the future. If you are at Peace, you are living in present. ~ Lao Tzu

2.3. What is Appreciation?

Peace comes from Within; therefore, it cannot be purchased. Peace, cannot be found outside of oneself, it dwells inside of ME but we must go to our deepest and darkest places of our souls and towards the Light of Whom I was created to be, not the person society has dictated me to be.

2.4. The Eight Steps of Atonement is a process to promote peace and to settle differences. Reconciliation with self and others and Responsibility for what you do and do not do.

1. Someone must point out the wrong
2. Acknowledgement of wrong
3. Confess the fault; first to Allah (God), then to those offended
4. Repentance; a feeling of remorse or contrition or shame for the past conduct which was wrong and sinful
5. Atonement; meaning to make amends and reparations for the wrong
6. Forgiveness by the offended party; to cease to feel offense and resentment against another for the harm done
7. Reconciliation and restoration; meaning to become friendly and peaceable again
8. Perfect union with Allah (God) and with each other

9. DEFINE PRO-SURVIVAL & CONTRA-SURVIVAL

9.1. Pro-Survival Definition

Pro-Survival means that aid in survival.

9.2. Contra-Survival Definition

Contra-Survival means doing something that flies in the face of common sense and is ultimately detrimental.

Are my thoughts towards ME, pro-survival or contra-survival?

_____

_____

_____

_____

_____

_____

List some pro-survival & contra-survival thoughts I have towards ME.

_____

_____

_____

_____

Will I be alright with what I have listed? What emotion is being invoked in ME?

_____

_____

_____

_____

_____

_____

How did my pro-survival/contra-survival make ME feel?

_____

_____

_____

_____

_____

_____

Why did I make the decision to be pro-survival/ contra-survival towards ME?

_____

_____

_____

_____

_____

_____

Where was I when I decided to be pro-survival/contra-survival?

_____

_____

_____

_____

_____

Who witnessed my pro-survival/contra-survival behavior?

_____

_____

_____

_____

Do I feel I owe them an explanation? Why/Why not?

_____

_____

_____

What measures will I put into place to be more pro-survival?

_____

_____

_____

_____

10. THE 10 SYSTEMS OF A UNIVERSAL ORDER

There are 9 Planets out here revolving around The Sun. These 9 Planets are mastered and controlled by The Light of The Sun, which keeps The Planets *in orbit* and *in order*. As long as The Planets obey The Law of Light, and keep within the prescribed limits of that Law, The Planets *function* well and there is *harmony* in The Universal Order.

The same thing applies to you and me.
Within the human being are **9 Functioning Systems**:
1) *Skeletal,* 2) *Digestive,* 3) *Lymphatic,* 4) *Muscle,* 5) *Respiratory,* 6) *Endocrine,* 7) *Nervous,* 8) *Circulatory* and 9) *Reproductive.*
And the **10th System** is **The Brain**.

Did you know that the health of this human body depends on how well these 10 Systems function in relationship to each other? Any time you get sick, there is a dis-order in the systems of your own body.

Now, this brain of ours is to be like "The Sun": It is to be *lit with Knowledge.* And by this brain being "lit with Knowledge, " then The Systems obey The Law of The Light of Our Knowledge, and we have harmony and order in The Function of Our Bodies.

But at the very moment our Light goes out in the 10th System, our Brain - the moment you do not have the kind of Knowledge that will allow you to live by The Divine Law of Almighty God - then because of **The Darkness of our thoughts** and **The Darkness**

our minds we begin to *interfere* with the harmonious function of our systems."

The Honorable Minister Louis Farrakhan
The Restrictive Law of Islam is Our Success, page 6 & 7

"Success is something you attract by the person you become. If you want to have more, you must become more." ~ Jim Rohn

"Greater is He that is in you, than he that is in the world."
1 John 4:4

11. QUESTION & ANSWERS

Who Am I going to become?

_____

_____

_____

_____

How does that make me feel?

_____

_____

_____

_____

Who will I leave behind in my BEcoming?

_____

_____

_____

_____

Will I be alright with that? What emotion is being invoked in ME?

_____

_____

_____

_____

12. QUESTION & ANSWERS

> "For whosoever shall do the will of my Father which is in heaven, the same is my brother and sister, and mother."
> Matthew 12:50.

So, what does that mean to ME?

_____

_____

_____

_____

_____

How does this make ME feel?

_____

_____

_____

_____

_____

_____

> .... Surely Allah changes not the condition of a people until they change their own condition. Holy Quran 13:11

"You have to want something for yourself and stop measuring your value through someone else's happiness. Just because you love someone does not mean their satisfaction automatically results in your satisfaction. You have to understand the difference."

Weapons of Self-Destruction
~ Ava Muhammad

FIRST

12-WEEK CHALLENGE

CHALLENGE 1

I AM Allah's (God's) greatest creation.
I AM more beautiful than a butterfly.
I AM allowing my transformation to BEgin!
~ *Karen Taylor Muhammad*

CALENDAR

Month/YEAR: _____

Sunday	Monday	Tuesday	Wednesday	Thursday	Friday	Saturday

THREE KEY ELEMENTS

SPIRITUAL:

_____
_____
_____
_____
_____

MIND/MENTAL:

_____
_____
_____
_____
_____

BODY/PHYSICAL:

_____
_____
_____
_____
_____

MY "ME" NOTES

My "ME" Notes Topic: _____

_____
_____
_____
_____
_____
_____
_____
_____
_____
_____
_____
_____
_____
_____
_____
_____
_____
_____
_____
_____
_____
_____

CHALLENGE 2

Searching for "ME", I must go through the darkest to find the Resonance Within. And I Will!
~ *Karen Taylor Muhammad*

CALENDAR

MONTH/YEAR: _____

Sunday	Monday	Tuesday	Wednesday	Thursday	Friday	Saturday

SELF-TRANSFORMATION
PART 1

Self

A person's essential being that distinguishes them from others, especially considered as the object of introspection or reflexive action.

Definitions from Oxford Languages

Self-Love

Regard for one's own well-being and happiness (chiefly considered as a desirable rather than narcissistic characteristic).

Definitions from Oxford Languages

Self-Awareness

Conscious knowledge of one's own character, feelings, motives, and desires.

Definitions from Oxford Languages

Self-Esteem

Confidence in one's own worth or abilities; self-respect.

Definitions from Oxford Languages

SELF Q & A

How do I see myself and Why?

_____

_____

_____

_____

_____

_____

_____

**Is my image defined by ME or someone?
If so, Who and Why?**

_____

_____

_____

_____

_____

_____

_____

_____

_____

_____

SELF-LOVE Q & A

Do I Love ME? Why or Why not?

_____

_____

_____

_____

_____

What is the root cause, I do not Love ME?

_____

_____

_____

_____

What is one love I now have for ME and Why?

_____

_____

_____

_____

"Love is the universal generator of life. It creates, sustains and nourishes everything in the Universe. This means all humans have a primary need for Love. At the core of your being is the impulse to share and receive this energy on its many levels through physical, mental, emotional and spiritual contact with others. This is not some vague, abstract idea; it is a substantive, magnetic energy."
~ Real Love, Ava Muhammad

SELF-AWARENESS Q & A

How do I feel about ME?

_____

_____

_____

_____

_____

_____

_____

_____

What desire do I have for ME?

_____

_____

_____

_____

_____

_____

_____

_____

_____

_____

_____

SELF-ESTEEM Q & A

What are my strengths?

_____

_____

_____

_____

_____

_____

_____

_____

Recall a time when I was confident in ME.

_____

_____

_____

_____

_____

_____

_____

_____

_____

_____

_____

MY "ME" NOTES

My "ME" Notes Topic: _____

_____

_____

_____

_____

_____

_____

_____

_____

_____

_____

_____

_____

_____

_____

_____

_____

_____

_____

_____

_____

_____

_____

_____

_____

My "ME" Notes Topics: _____

_____

_____

_____

_____

_____

_____

_____

_____

_____

_____

_____

_____

_____

_____

_____

_____

_____

_____

_____

_____

_____

_____

_____

_____

CHALLENGE 3

The War Within is Real; Only ME (Light) and/or ME
(Darkness) get to decide who wins.
~ *Karen Taylor Muhammad*

CALENDAR

MONTH/YEAR: _____

Sunday	Monday	Tuesday	Wednesday	Thursday	Friday	Saturday

SELF-TRANSFORMATION
PART 2

Self-Discipline

The ability to control one's feelings and overcome one's weaknesses; the ability to pursue what one thinks is right despite temptations to abandon it.

Definitions from Oxford Languages

Self-Control

The ability to control oneself, in particular one's emotions and desires or the expression of them in one's behavior, especially in difficult situations.

Definitions from Oxford Languages

Unity

The state of being united or joined as a whole.

Definitions from Oxford Languages

SELF-DISCIPLINE Q & A

How often do I show up for ME?

_____

_____

_____

_____

_____

_____

_____

Why don't I show up for ME daily?

_____

_____

_____

_____

_____

_____

When I do show up for ME, how does that make ME feel?

_____

_____

_____

_____

_____

SELF-CONTROL Q & A

Am I proactive or reactive?

_____

_____

_____

_____

When I'm proactive, who's in control?

_____

_____

_____

_____

When I'm reactive, who's in control?

_____

_____

_____

_____

How do I have control over it?

_____

_____

_____

_____

UNITY Q & A

AM I in unity with ME?

_____
_____
_____
_____
_____
_____
_____

Why or Why not?

_____
_____
_____
_____
_____
_____

How do I become in Unity with ME?

_____
_____
_____
_____
_____

MY "ME" NOTES

_____

_____

_____

_____

_____

_____

_____

_____

_____

_____

_____

_____

_____

_____

_____

_____

_____

_____

_____

_____

_____

_____

_____

My "ME" Notes Topic: _____

_____

_____

_____

_____

_____

_____

_____

_____

_____

_____

_____

_____

_____

_____

_____

_____

_____

_____

_____

_____

_____

_____

My "ME" Notes Topic: _____

CHALLENGE 4

The war within is real and constant; yet, I AM persistently settling on ME (Light). Where there is PEACE!
~ *Karen Taylor Muhammad*

CALENDAR

MONTH/YEAR: _____

Sunday	Monday	Tuesday	Wednesday	Thursday	Friday	Saturday

ESSAY CHALLENGE

Who you are now:

_____

_____

_____

_____

_____

_____

_____

_____

_____

_____

_____

_____

_____

_____

_____

_____

_____

_____

_____

_____

_____

Who you would like to be at the end of the 12 weeks / 3 months?

_____

_____

_____

_____

_____

_____

_____

_____

_____

_____

_____

_____

_____

_____

_____

_____

_____

_____

_____

_____

_____

_____

MY "ME" NOTES

My "ME" Notes Topic: _____

_____

_____

_____

_____

_____

_____

_____

_____

_____

_____

_____

_____

_____

_____

_____

_____

_____

_____

_____

_____

_____

_____

_____

My "ME" Notes Topic: _____

_____

_____

_____

_____

_____

_____

_____

_____

_____

_____

_____

_____

_____

_____

_____

_____

_____

_____

_____

_____

_____

_____

_____

SECOND
12-WEEK CHALLENGE

CHALLENGE 5

Gratitude allows ME to see beauty everywhere.
And then PEACE is everywhere I AM.
~ *Karen Taylor Muhammad*

CALENDAR

Month/YEAR: _____

Sunday	Monday	Tuesday	Wednesday	Thursday	Friday	Saturday

THREE KEY ELEMENTS

SPIRITUAL:

_____

MIND/MENTAL:

_____

BODY/PHYSICAL:

_____

MY "ME" NOTES

My "ME" Notes: _____

_____

_____

_____

_____

_____

_____

_____

_____

_____

_____

_____

_____

_____

_____

_____

_____

_____

_____

_____

_____

_____

_____

CHALLENGE 6

Solitude allows ME to hear the Resonance Within.
~ *Karen Taylor Muhammad*

CALENDAR

MONTH/YEAR: _____

Sunday	Monday	Tuesday	Wednesday	Thursday	Friday	Saturday

SELF-TRANSFORMATION
PART 1

Self

A person's essential being that distinguishes them from others, especially considered as the object of introspection or reflexive action.

Definitions from Oxford Languages

Self-Love

Regard for one's own well-being and happiness (chiefly considered as a desirable rather than narcissistic characteristic).

Definitions from Oxford Languages

Self-Awareness

Conscious knowledge of one's own character, feelings, motives, and desires.

Definitions from Oxford Languages

Self-Esteem

Confidence in one's own worth or abilities; self-respect.

Definitions from Oxford Languages

SELF Q & A

How do I see myself and Why?

_____
_____
_____
_____
_____
_____
_____
_____

Is myself image defined by ME or someone?
If so, Who and Why?

_____
_____
_____
_____
_____
_____
_____
_____
_____
_____
_____

SELF-LOVE Q & A

Do I Love ME? Why or Why not?

_____

_____

_____

_____

_____

What is the root cause, I do not Love ME?

_____

_____

_____

_____

What is one love I now have for ME and Why?

_____

_____

_____

_____

"The spiritual journey does not consist in arriving at a new destination where a person gains what he does not have, or becomes what he is not. It consists in the dissipation of one's own ignorance concerning one's self and life, and the gradual growth of that understanding, which begins the spiritual awakening. The finding of God is a coming to one's self."

~ _Aldous Huxley_

SELF-AWARENESS Q & A

How do I feel about ME?

_____
_____
_____
_____
_____
_____
_____

What desire do I have for ME?

_____
_____
_____
_____
_____
_____
_____
_____
_____
_____
_____

SELF-ESTEEM Q & A

What are my strengths?

_____
_____
_____
_____
_____
_____
_____
_____

Recall a time when I was confident in ME.

_____
_____
_____
_____
_____
_____
_____
_____
_____
_____
_____

MY "ME" NOTES

My "ME" Notes Topic: _____

_____

_____

_____

_____

_____

_____

_____

_____

_____

_____

_____

_____

_____

_____

_____

_____

_____

_____

_____

_____

_____

_____

_____

My "ME" Notes Topic: _____

_____

_____

_____

_____

_____

_____

_____

_____

_____

_____

_____

_____

_____

_____

_____

_____

_____

_____

_____

_____

_____

_____

CHALLENGE 7

Life's storms & Life's calmness (ease) are
for a reason and a season.
AM I learning Life's Lessons in them?
~ *Karen Taylor Muhammad*

CALENDAR

MONTH/YEAR: _____

Sunday	Monday	Tuesday	Wednesday	Thursday	Friday	Saturday

SELF-TRANSFORMATION
PART 2

Self-Discipline

The ability to control one's feelings and overcome one's weaknesses; the ability to pursue what one thinks is right despite temptations to abandon it.

Definitions from Oxford Languages

Self-Control

The ability to control oneself, in particular one's emotions and desires or the expression of them in one's behavior, especially in difficult situations.

Definitions from Oxford Languages

Unity

The state of being united or joined as a whole.

Definitions from Oxford Languages

SELF-DISCIPLINE Q & A

How often do I show up for ME?

_____
_____
_____
_____
_____
_____
_____

Why don't I show up for ME daily?

_____
_____
_____
_____
_____
_____

When I do show up for ME, how does that make ME feel?

_____
_____
_____
_____
_____

SELF-CONTROL Q & A

Am I proactive or reactive?

_____

_____

_____

_____

When I'm proactive who's in control?

_____

_____

_____

_____

When I'm reactive who's in control?

_____

_____

_____

_____

How do I have control over it?

_____

_____

_____

_____

UNITY Q & A

AM I in unity with ME?

_____
_____
_____
_____
_____
_____
_____

Why or Why not?

_____
_____
_____
_____
_____
_____

How do I become in Unity with ME?

_____
_____
_____
_____
_____

MY "ME" NOTES

My "ME" Notes Topic: _____

_____

_____

_____

_____

_____

_____

_____

_____

_____

_____

_____

_____

_____

_____

_____

_____

_____

_____

_____

_____

_____

_____

_____

_____

_____

My "ME" Notes Topics: _____

_____

_____

_____

_____

_____

_____

_____

_____

_____

_____

_____

_____

_____

_____

_____

_____

_____

_____

_____

_____

_____

_____

_____

CHALLENGE 8

The Resonance Within shines brightly.
I AM setting ME free!!
~ *Karen Taylor Muhammad*

CALENDAR

MONTH/YEAR: _____

Sunday	Monday	Tuesday	Wednesday	Thursday	Friday	Saturday

ESSAY CHALLENGE

Who you are now:

_____
_____
_____
_____
_____
_____
_____
_____
_____
_____
_____
_____
_____
_____
_____
_____
_____
_____
_____
_____
_____
_____
_____

Who you would like to be at the end of the 12 weeks / 3 months?

_____

_____

_____

_____

_____

_____

_____

_____

_____

_____

_____

_____

_____

_____

_____

_____

_____

_____

_____

_____

_____

_____

MY "ME" NOTES

My "ME" Notes Topic: _____

_____

_____

_____

_____

_____

_____

_____

_____

_____

_____

_____

_____

_____

_____

_____

_____

_____

_____

_____

_____

_____

_____

_____

My "ME" Notes Topic: _____

_____

_____

_____

_____

_____

_____

_____

_____

_____

_____

_____

_____

_____

_____

_____

_____

_____

_____

_____

_____

_____

THIRD

12-WEEK CHALLENGE

CHALLENGE 9

I AM a light that can no longer be hindered
(impeded) nor hidden (concealed).
~ *Karen Taylor Muhammad*

CALENDAR

Month/YEAR: _____

Sunday	Monday	Tuesday	Wednesday	Thursday	Friday	Saturday

THREE KEY ELEMENTS

SPIRITUAL:

```
_____
_____
_____
_____
_____
_____
```

MIND/MENTAL:

```
_____
_____
_____
_____
_____
```

BODY/PHYSICAL:

```
_____
_____
_____
_____
_____
```

MY "ME" NOTES

My "ME" Notes Topic: _____

_____

_____

_____

_____

_____

_____

_____

_____

_____

_____

_____

_____

_____

_____

_____

_____

_____

_____

_____

_____

CHALLENGE 10

I AM the beauty in the haze awaiting for ME to discover.
~ Karen Taylor Muhammad

CALENDAR

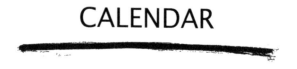

MONTH/YEAR: _____

Sunday	Monday	Tuesday	Wednesday	Thursday	Friday	Saturday

SELF-TRANSFORMATION
PART 1

Self

A person's essential being that distinguishes them from others, especially considered as the object of introspection or reflexive action.

Definitions from Oxford Languages

Self-Love

Regard for one's own well-being and happiness (chiefly considered as a desirable rather than narcissistic characteristic).

Definitions from Oxford Languages

Self-Awareness

Conscious knowledge of one's own character, feelings, motives, and desires.

Definitions from Oxford Languages

Self-Esteem

Confidence in one's own worth or abilities; self-respect.

Definitions from Oxford Languages

SELF Q & A

How do I see myself and Why?

_____

_____

_____

_____

_____

_____

_____

_____

**Is my self-image defined by ME or someone?
If so, Who and Why?**

_____

_____

_____

_____

_____

_____

_____

_____

_____

_____

_____

SELF-LOVE Q & A

Do I Love ME? Why or Why not?

_____

_____

_____

_____

_____

What is the root cause, I do not Love ME?

_____

_____

_____

_____

_____

What is one love I now have for ME and Why?

_____

_____

_____

_____

_____

"Surrender is a journey from the outer turmoil to the inner peace." ~ _Sri Chinmoy_

SELF-AWARENESS Q & A

How do I feel about ME?

What desire do I have for ME?

SELF-ESTEEM Q & A

What are my strengths?

_____

_____

_____

_____

_____

_____

_____

_____

Recall a time when I was confident in ME.

_____

_____

_____

_____

_____

_____

_____

_____

_____

_____

_____

MY "ME" NOTES

My "ME" Notes Topic: _____

_____

_____

My "ME" Notes Topic: _____

_____

_____

_____

_____

_____

_____

_____

_____

_____

_____

_____

_____

_____

_____

_____

_____

_____

_____

_____

_____

_____

_____

_____

CHALLENGE 11

Surrender is the journey to the Peace Within ME.
~ Karen Taylor Muhammad

CALENDAR

MONTH/YEAR: _____

Sunday	Monday	Tuesday	Wednesday	Thursday	Friday	Saturday

SELF-TRANSFORMATION
PART 2

Self-Discipline

The ability to control one's feelings and overcome one's weaknesses; the ability to pursue what one thinks is right despite temptations to abandon it.

Definitions from Oxford Languages

Self-Control

The ability to control oneself, in particular one's emotions and desires or the expression of them in one's behavior, especially in difficult situations.

Definitions from Oxford Languages

Unity

The state of being united or joined as a whole.

Definitions from Oxford Languages

SELF-DISCIPLINE Q & A

How often do I show up for ME?

_____
_____
_____
_____
_____
_____
_____

Why don't I show up for ME daily?

_____
_____
_____
_____
_____
_____

When I do show up for ME, how does that make ME feel?

_____
_____
_____
_____
_____

SELF-CONTROL Q & A

Am I proactive or reactive?

_____
_____
_____
_____

When I'm proactive, who's in control?

_____
_____
_____
_____

When I'm reactive, who's in control?

_____
_____
_____
_____

How do I have control over it?

_____
_____
_____
_____

UNITY Q & A

AM I in unity with ME?

_____
_____
_____
_____
_____
_____

Why or Why not?

_____
_____
_____
_____
_____
_____

How do I become in Unity with ME?

_____
_____
_____
_____

MY "ME" NOTES

_____
_____
_____
_____
_____
_____
_____
_____
_____
_____
_____
_____
_____
_____
_____
_____
_____
_____
_____
_____
_____
_____
_____
_____
_____

My "ME" Notes Topic: _____

_____
_____
_____
_____
_____
_____
_____
_____
_____
_____
_____
_____
_____
_____
_____
_____
_____
_____
_____
_____
_____
_____
_____
_____

My "ME" Notes Topic: _____

_____
_____
_____
_____
_____
_____
_____
_____
_____
_____
_____
_____
_____
_____
_____
_____
_____
_____
_____
_____
_____
_____

CHALLENGE 12

I AM all that Allah (God) created ME to BE.
I AM one with HIM!
~ *Karen Taylor Muhammad*

CALENDAR

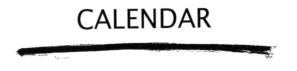

MONTH/YEAR: _____

Sunday	Monday	Tuesday	Wednesday	Thursday	Friday	Saturday

ESSAY CHALLENGE

Who you are now:

_____

_____

_____

_____

_____

_____

_____

_____

_____

_____

_____

_____

_____

_____

_____

_____

_____

_____

_____

_____

_____

_____

_____

Who you would like to be at the end of the 12 weeks / 3 months?

MY "ME" NOTES

My "ME" Notes Topic: _____

_____

_____

_____

_____

_____

_____

_____

_____

_____

_____

_____

_____

_____

_____

_____

_____

_____

_____

_____

_____

_____

_____

_____

My "ME" Notes Topic: _____

_____

_____

_____

_____

_____

_____

_____

_____

_____

_____

_____

_____

_____

_____

_____

_____

_____

_____

_____

_____

_____

RESOURCES
12-WEEK JOURNAL

LETTER

I'M BEING MADE NEW

Because of you, I 've been Made New; Thank you!!...I'm grateful!!

We met, you made promises and deep within I knew you couldn't keep.

I heard your voice louder than I heard my own' talking swiftly with deceit.

You didn't listen to me when I told you I couldn't be the woman you needed me to be. Your needs were your only concern and you convinced me that they were mine, again in deceit.

You said, when God made you, He was thinking about me and I started to believe that when God made me, He was thinking about you.

You shared your story many times about a lie walking in truth clothing. Later, I realized that the lie was you walking in human form.

You said, "I need your strength", and I gave it to you, ignoring my own needs until you almost destroyed me.

I am no longer angry, scared, insecure, disappointed, or lonely.

I have forgiven myself and I forgave you.

Because of you I've been Made New; Thank you!!

Now I know, when God created Me, He was thinking only of Me.

Respectfully,

Karen Taylor Muhammad

RESOURCES

The Holy Quran (Maulana Muhammad Ali)

The Bible (King James Version)

Message To The Blackman In America - Elijah Muhammad

Restrictive Laws of Islam is Our Success - The Honorable Minister Louis Farrakhan (THMLF)

Self-Improvement is the Basis of Community Development – The Honorable Minister Louis Farrakhan (THMLF)

Closing the Gap - Jabril Muhammad

Weapons of Self-Destruction, Real Love, A New Way of Life, Force and Power of Being, Naturally Beautiful – Ava Muhammad

What the Beep Do We Know!?

The Matrix Movies

The Secret of Infatuation – Deepa Chopra – The Secret of Love: Mediation for Attracting & Being Love

Will – Deepa Chopra, Paul Avgerinos & Kabir Sehgal – Spiritual Warrior

Opposition - The Soul of Healing Affirmations – A-Z Guide to Reprogramming the Software of the Soul- Deepa Chopra & Adam Plack

The Fifth Law - Surrender - Deepa Chopra & Adam Plank - A Gift of Love

The Law of Dharma - Deepak Chopra, Paul Avgerinos & Kabir Sehgal _Musical Mediation on The Seven Spirituals Laws of Success

Dianetic -The Modern Science of Mental Health, A New Slant of Life, Self -Analysis, Science of Survival, The Original Thesis, The Fundamental of Thought, The Ethics Book - L. Ron Hubbard

The Power of the Subconscious Mind – Joseph Murphy

The Twelve Universal Laws of Success – Herbert Harris

The Way Out, The Impersonal Life – Unknown Author

The Art of War -Sun Tzu

Abraham Hicks

The Moment, Goodbye is a New Beginning, Silence, Warrior –
Songs by Vargo

"I would rather regret doing than not doing that way
I would know!" ~ Karen Taylor Muhammad

CONTACT

Karen Taylor Muhammad
(919) 758-9625
ResonanceWithin.KTM@gmail.com

International Sports Science Association (ISSA) Certified:
Corrective Exercise Specialist,
Personal Trainer & Fitness Coach

ISSA Pending Certification:
Online Coaching, Yoga, Nutritionist & Health Coach

Experiences:
Competitive Powerlifter,
Competitive Bodybuilder & CrossFit Coach
Law Enforcement Official, Crime Prevention Specialist,
Professional Truck Driver/ Owner Operator,
Restaurant Services, Mortgage Specialist

Join the "ME" Project – Challenges
Recurring: Every 12 Weeks/ 3 Months
Email Your request to join
ResonanceWithin.KTM@gmail.com